Read-About® Geography

Mount Everest

By Sarah De Capua

Consultant
Linda Cornwell
National Literacy Specialist

Children's Press®
A Division of Scholastic Inc.
New York   Toronto   London   Auckland   Sydney
Mexico City   New Delhi   Hong Kong
Danbury, Connecticut

Designer: Herman Adler Design
Photo Researcher: Caroline Anderson
The photo on the cover shows Mount Everest.

Library of Congress Cataloging-in-Publication Data

De Capua, Sarah.
    Mount Everest/ by Sarah De Capua
      p. cm. — (Rookie read-about geography)
    Includes index.
    ISBN 0-516-22015-2 (lib. bdg.)   0-516-27391-4 (pbk.)
    1. Everest, Mount (China and Nepal)—Juvenile literature.
  [1. Everest, Mount (China and Nepal)] I. Title. II. Series.

DS495.8.E9 D4   2002
954.9'6—dc21

                             00-031391

Have you ever played king of the mountain?

A mountain is a very high piece of land. You can find mountains all over the world.

Mount Everest (EV-uhr-ist) is the highest mountain on Earth. It is 29,035 feet high. That's about as high as most big airplanes fly!

Mount Everest is found
between Tibet and Nepal
on the continent of Asia.

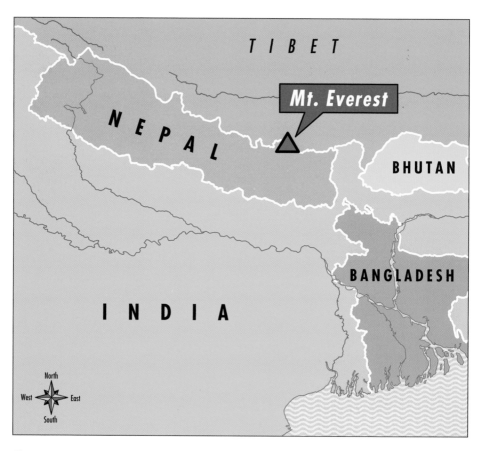

It is part of a group
of mountains called the
Himalayas (him–uh–LAY–uhs).

Mount Everest is covered with snow all year.

12

It is also covered with glaciers. Glaciers are huge rivers of ice.

Mount Everest is very cold. Only a few animals and plants can live there.

People called Sherpas
(SHUR-puhs) live
in Nepal.

Many Sherpas work
as guides.

They help mountain climbers reach the top of Mount Everest.

Mountain climbers come from all over the world to climb this famous mountain.

It is difficult to climb
Mount Everest.

Many mountain climbers
have died trying to reach
the top.

But hundreds of mountain climbers have been successful.

The first people reached the top of Mount Everest in 1953.

They were Sir Edmund Hillary and his Sherpa guide, Tenzing Norgay.

Can you imagine standing on top of the highest mountain in the world?

Words You Know

glacier

Himalayas

Mount Everest

mountain

mountain climber

Sherpas

Index

About the Author

Sarah De Capua is an author and editor of children's books. She resides in Colorado.

Photo Credits

Photographs © 2002: Archive Photos/Getty Images/Reuters/HO: 25; Corbis-Bettmann/Galen Rowell: 18, 22; Earth Scenes/Michael Andrews: 9, 30 bottom; First Light/D. Keaton: 29; Liaison Agency, Inc./Getty Images/Nova Online: cover, 19; National Geographic Image Collection/Bobby Model: 21, 31 bottom left; Photo Researchers, NY/Art Twomey: 15; Stone/Getty Images/Nicholas DeVore: 12, 30 top; Superstock, Inc.: 3 (William Prosor), 4, 7, 31 top left, 31 top right; The Image Works: 11 (DPA), 26 (Topham), 16, 31 bottom right (Alison Wright).

Map by Bob Italiano